The Spanish Missions of Arizona

ROBIN LYON

Children's Press®
An Imprint of Scholastic Inc.
New York Toronto London Auckland Sydney
Mexico City New Delhi Hong Kong
Danbury, Connecticut

Content Consultant
Kristina W. Foss
Museum Director, Santa Barbara Mission Museum

Library of Congress Cataloging-in-Publication Data

Lyon, Robin.
  The Spanish missions of Arizona / by Robin Lyon.
      p. cm.—(A true book)
  Includes bibliographical references and index.
  ISBN-13: 978-0-531-20576-1 (lib. bdg.)   978-0-531-21239-4 (pbk.)
  ISBN-10: 0-531-20576-2 (lib. bdg.)   0-531-21239-4 (pbk.)

1. Arizona—History—To 1912—Juvenile literature. 2. Missions,
Spanish—Arizona—History—Juvenile literature. 3. Indians of North
America—Missions—Arizona—Juvenile literature. 4. Franciscans—
Missions—Arizona—History—Juvenile literature. I. Title. II. Series.

F811.L866 2010
979.1'02—dc22   200901841

1 2 3 4 5 6 7 8 9 10 R 19 18 17 16 15 14 13 12 11 10   62

Find the Truth!

Everything you are about to read is true *except* for one of the sentences on this page.

Which one is **TRUE**?

T or F   Native Americans in Arizona welcomed the Spanish missions.

T or F   Spanish explorers searched Arizona for a city of gold.

Find the answers in this book.

Contents

Great Horned Owl

The Apache were a strong people who fought to keep their land.

Bell at Mission San
José de Tumacácori

Mission San José de Tumacácori (SAN ho-SAY DAY too-mah-KAH-kore-ee) was founded in 1691.

CHAPTER 1

On a Mission

Catholic priests from Spain began setting up missions in what is now the state of Arizona in the 1600s. Missions were small villages that the priests started in areas where Native Americans lived. The priests wanted to **convert** the Native peoples to Christianity and make them live more like Spanish people did in Europe.

Mission San José de Tumacácori was the first mission in southern Arizona.

New Land for Spain

Christopher Columbus led a group of Spanish explorers to the Americas in 1492. The Spanish soon **claimed** Mexico, Peru, and many Caribbean islands as their own. In the mid-1500s, Spanish explorers began traveling north from Mexico into what is now the southwestern United States.

With Catholic priests, they set up missions—first in New Mexico and later in Arizona, Texas, and California.

Spain conquered Mexico in 1521.

Missionary Work

The missions were the first Spanish settlements in the southwestern United States.

The priests at these missions were called **missionaries**. They worked to get Native Americans to accept the Christian religion and European ways of life.

Soldiers and priests traveled together to start missions.

The missionaries also introduced cattle, sheep, and European fruits and vegetables to the region.

Native Americans in Arizona had never seen horses until the Spanish arrived with them.

9

CHAPTER 2

Inside Arizona

In 1539, a priest named Marcos de Niza led a group north from Mexico into what is now Arizona. De Niza was looking for amazing cities that were the focus of a Spanish legend. The legend told of seven cities of gold that lay north of Mexico. When he returned to Mexico, de Niza reported that he had seen a large city full of riches.

Traveling from central Mexico to Arizona took Spanish explorers as long as two or three months.

Coronado traveled through Arizona with more than 1,600 people.

Spanish Journeys

In 1540, explorer Francisco Vázquez de Coronado (VAS-kes DAY kor-oh-NAH-doh) searched Arizona for these cities of gold but found nothing. For the next 40 years, the Spanish lost interest in Arizona.

Then, in 1583, Antonio de Espejo (ess-PAY-ho) explored northern Arizona. There he discovered silver and copper, and claimed the land for Spain. Espejo's discoveries renewed Spain's interest in Arizona. Soon after, the Spanish began setting up mines and missions in the area.

Native Americans and Spanish Meet

Once the Spanish began setting up missions, they met several groups of Native Americans who called the region home. These Native peoples lived in the Sonoran (suh-NORE-un) Desert, in what is now southern Arizona, and along the Santa Cruz and San Pedro rivers. The Spanish missionaries set up missions in these areas. Native peoples were expected to live and work at the missions while the missionaries tried to convert them to Christianity.

UTAH

NEVADA

N

0   50 mi.
0   50 km

ARIZONA

NEW MEXICO

CALIFORNIA

Colorado R.

Phoenix

Gila R.

Gila R.

Santa Cruz R.

SONORAN DESERT

Tucson

San Xavier del Bac

San José de Tumacácori

San Cayetano de Calabazas

Los Santos Ángeles de Guevavi

MEXICO

Tumacácori National Historic Park

Nogales

KEY
- Mission
- Pimería Alta
- Present-day border
- Present-day city

The Hopi and Apache

Two of the largest Native groups in Arizona at this time were the Hopi (HO-pee) and the Apache (uh-PAH-chee). The Hopi lived in towns in what is now northern Arizona. They sometimes guided early Spanish explorers around the region. Many Hopi refused to convert to Christianity. The Apache were **nomadic** people who lived farther south and west. They often attacked the missions, trying to force the Spanish people away. Neither group wanted to give up their traditional religions or ways of life.

Hopi women weaving baskets

14

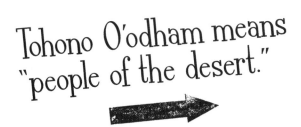

Tohono O'odham means "people of the desert."

The Tohono O'odham

In the Sonoran Desert, Spanish missionaries met the Tohono O'odham (toe-HO-no AH-tomb) people. Many Tohono O'odham lived at the missions. They were more willing to work with the missionaries than other Native groups in Arizona. Away from the missions, some early Spanish settlers enslaved the Tohono O'odham, forcing them to work in silver mines.

The Tohono O'odham's homes in the Pimería Alta were made of trees, grass, and dirt.

The Pimería Alta

Many of the Tohono O'odham people, as well as other Native groups, lived in a region that the Spanish called the Pimería Alta (pee-mare-EE-ah AL-tah). This area stretched from southern Arizona to northern Mexico. In the late 1600s, Father Eusebio Kino (yoo-SEB-yo KEE-no), an Italian-born missionary, started an important group of missions in the Pimería Alta.

A Missionary and More

Father Kino started more than 20 missions in Arizona and Mexico. One of these, San José de Tumacácori, was the first mission in southern Arizona. Father Kino had a good relationship with the Tohono O'odham and learned their language. He tried to stop the Spanish from forcing Native peoples to work in silver mines. Father Kino was also a skilled **mathematician** (math-uh-muh-TI-shun) and mapmaker.

Father Kino served as a missionary in the Pimería Alta for 28 years.

The presidio at Tubac was built in 1752.

Bill Ahrendt

CHAPTER 3

Mission Life

The Spanish built a chain of missions across southern Arizona. Near some missions, they built **presidios** (preh-SEE-dee-ohz), or forts. The presidios housed soldiers who helped protect people living at the missions. Each mission included a church, a school, places for the missionaries and Native peoples to sleep, and farmland.

← Tubac was the site of the first presidio in Arizona.

Brick by Brick

Native Americans usually built the mission churches. Mission priests and Spanish workers planned the design. Few trees grow in the hot, dry Sonoran Desert, so there was very little wood to use in building the churches. Instead, most mission churches there were built of **adobe** (uh-DOH-bee) bricks. The mission walls were plastered and sometimes painted white. The juice of the prickly pear cactus was often used to make the plaster that held the bricks in place.

Even in the hot desert, adobe bricks keep the heat out of buildings.

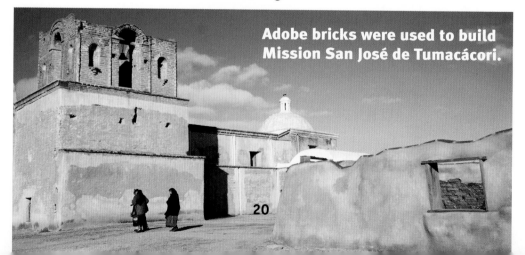

Adobe bricks were used to build Mission San José de Tumacácori.

Mission bells rang to announce when it was time to work, eat, and pray.

Hard Work

The missions included ranches and farms that provided food for everyone living there. Native people planted and harvested the crops, and took care of the cattle, sheep, and other animals. They also cooked meals and made clothes and other goods. But Native people were rarely paid for their work.

The Sonoran Desert

Many of the Spanish missions in Arizona were located in the Sonoran Desert. This desert stretches across southwestern Arizona and southeastern California, and extends south into the state of Sonora in northern Mexico. Of all the deserts in the world, the Sonoran Desert is home to the widest variety of plants and animals.

Saguaro Cactus

Many types of cactus grow in the Sonoran Desert, including the tall saguaro (sa-WAR-ah) cactus. The saguaro's blossom is the state flower of Arizona.

Rattlesnake

Six kinds of rattlesnakes live in Arizona's Sonoran Desert. They get their name from the rattle at the end of their tails, which they shake as a warning when they feel threatened.

Great Horned Owl

This large owl does not actually have horns. It gets its name from the tufts of feathers on top of its head. Great horned owls usually hunt in the cool of the night. They eat rabbits, squirrels, mice, and other small animals.

CHAPTER 4

Worlds Collide

At times, the Spanish missionaries and the Native Americans in Arizona came into conflict. The Spanish often forced Native people to work and treated them cruelly. The Native people had their own long-held religious beliefs. The Spanish wanted to make them give up their beliefs and become Christian. For all of these reasons, Native people sometimes attacked the missions, trying to drive the Spanish off their land.

← The Apache people first got horses from the Spanish.

The Hopi Rise Up

In the 1500s, the Spanish tried to establish missions in what is now northern Arizona, where many Hopi people lived. But the Hopi did not welcome the Spanish, and the missions failed. In 1629, the Spanish tried again, founding missions closer to Hopi villages. These missions survived until 1680, when the Hopi drove the Spanish missionaries out of the area for good.

Some Hopi villages that still stand today in Arizona are more than 800 years old.

The Spanish abandoned some missions because of Apache attacks.

The Apache Fight Back

The Apache were not happy about the Spanish missions taking over their land. They attacked the missions regularly to defend their territory. They also attacked the Tohono O'odham people because some of them helped protect the Spanish from the Apache attacks.

The Pima Revolts

The Tohono O'odham rose up against the Spanish twice in what are called the Pima **Revolts**. The first revolt took place in 1695 as the Spanish took over Tohono O'odham land. The missions survived this revolt, and Father Kino helped bring back peace to the region.

The second revolt, in 1751, was more serious. It was led by Luis Oacpicagigua (loo-EES wok-peek-ah-GEE-gwah), a Tohono O'odham soldier. The revolt began when Native people killed 18 Spanish settlers at Oacpicagigua's home. During the next three months, he and his followers attacked the homes of Spanish settlers. More than 100 settlers were killed. Eventually, the Spanish army put an end to the revolt.

It took Spanish soldiers three months to end the second Pima Revolt.

More than 90,000 adobe bricks were used to build the Tumacácori mission church.

CHAPTER 5

Missions Across Arizona

Mission San José de Tumacácori was the first mission built in southern Arizona. Father Kino founded it in 1691. The mission was first located on the east side of the Santa Cruz River. Following the Pima Revolt of 1751, the mission was moved across the Santa Cruz close to Nogales, Arizona. A new, larger church that was built in the 1800s is now part of Tumacácori National Historical Park.

Mission Los Santos Ángeles de Guevavi

Mission Los Santos Ángeles de Guevavi (gay-VAH-vee) was founded only one day after Mission San José de Tumacácori. The mission faced many problems. Disease killed many of the Native people who lived there. The Pima Revolt and Apache attacks also took the lives of soldiers who guarded the mission. Mission Los Santos Ángeles de Guevavi was finally abandoned in 1775.

Guevavi comes from an O'odham word meaning "big well."

Mission Los Santos Ángeles de Guevavi was located near Nogales, Arizona, just north of what is now the U.S.–Mexico border.

A cover protects the ruins at Mission San Cayetano de Calabazas.

Mission San Cayetano de Calabazas

In 1756, Mission San Cayetano de Calabazas (kah-yeh-TAH-no DAY kah-lah-BAH-sahs) was founded in southern Arizona. Several Tohono O'odham people lived at the mission, but it was abandoned after only 30 years. The land was later used as a farm for Mission San José de Tumacácori from 1807 to 1830. Today, nothing remains but ruins of some of the buildings.

The current San Xavier del Bac church was built between 1783 and 1797.

Mission San Xavier del Bac

Father Kino founded Mission San Xavier del Bac (hav-EE-air DEL BAHK) in 1700, just outside what is now the city of Tucson. *Del Bac* means "place where water appears." The mission was given this name because the Santa Cruz River comes up from underground near it. The church is known for its beautifully decorated interior.

Art at San Xavier del Bac

The inside of Mission San Xavier del Bac is as beautiful as the outside. It is filled with twisting, carved columns, statues dressed in clothes, and lush paintings. Every inch of the **altar** is painted in bright colors. Native artists created most of the carvings and other decorations for the church. Through the years, the art at San Xavier del Bac was damaged, but now it is being repaired.

Most of the carvings in San Xavier del Bac are made of wood.

35

CHAPTER 6

Changing Times

Few of the missions in Arizona lasted more than 100 years. The spread of European diseases killed many Native people living at the missions. Attacks by Native Americans destroyed many mission buildings. The attacks forced other missions to be abandoned as people left to avoid being killed. Still other missions closed because so many Native Americans in the area had converted to Christianity that the missions were no longer necessary.

By 1850, San Xavier del Bac was the only active mission remaining in Arizona.

Spanish Diseases

The missionaries and explorers brought with them diseases common in Europe, such as measles

Thousands of Native people in Arizona died from smallpox and measles.

and smallpox. Native Americans had never before been exposed to these diseases, and their bodies could not fight them. Because of this, diseases spread quickly, and many people died.

Timeline of the Arizona Missions

1539
Father Marcos de Niza leads Spanish explorers into Arizona.

1691
Father Kino starts the first Spanish mission in southern Arizona.

Missions Today

Little remains of the Arizona missions built by Father Kino and others. Most of them slowly fell apart after they were

Children prepare for a service at Mission San Xavier del Bac.

abandoned. Parts of old stone and adobe walls are all that remains of most of the Arizona missions. San Xavier del Bac, near the city of Tucson, is the one mission that still exists today with an active church.

1797

The current San Xavier del Bac church is completed.

1751

The Tohono O'odham revolt against the missions.

Tumacácori National Historical Park preserves the ruins of three missions.

Saving the Missions

Today, the ruins of Missions San José de Tumacácori, Los Santos Ángeles de Guevavi, and San Cayetano de Calabazas are protected by Tumacácori National Historical Park in southern Arizona. Each of these missions was established by Father Kino. Every year, the National Park Service works to take care of and repair these buildings so they will continue to look as they once did.

Alive and Well

Mission San Xavier del Bac still serves the Tohono O'odham community in Arizona today. The O'odham who now attend the mission's church are the relatives of the people who actually helped to build it hundreds of years ago.

Each year, many people visit the Arizona missions. By touring San Xavier del Bac and long-abandoned missions, visitors learn how the Native peoples and the missionaries lived and worked at the Arizona missions.

San Xavier del Bac

41

Leaving Their Mark

The Spanish missions had a huge influence on Arizona and other parts of the United States. The missionaries brought new animals and crops to the area. They brought to the region the Spanish language, which is still spoken by many people throughout Arizona. They also introduced Mexican foods to Arizona. Many of these foods are still enjoyed by people in Arizona today. ★

Some women in Arizona cook tortillas in the traditional way.

True Statistics

First mission founded in Arizona: San José de Tumacácori in 1691

Number of missions founded by Father Kino: More than 20 in Arizona and Mexico

Number of missions in Tumacácori National Historical Park: 3

Size of the Sonoran Desert: 120,000 square miles (more than 310,000 square kilometers)

Number of types of plants in the Sonoran Desert: More than 2,000

Did you find the truth?

(F) Native Americans welcomed the Spanish missions.

(T) Spanish explorers searched Arizona for a city of gold.

Resources

Books

Bial, Raymond. *Missions and Presidios.* New York: Children's Press, 2004.

Ditchfield, Christin. *Spanish Missions.* New York: Children's Press, 2006.

Drain, Thomas. *A Sense of Mission: Historic Churches of the Southwest.* San Francisco: Chronicle Books, 1994.

Durrett, Deanne. *Arizona* (Seeds of a Nation). San Diego: Kidhaven, 2003.

Kalman, Bobbie. *Spanish Missions.* New York: Crabtree Publishing Company, 1997.

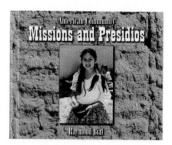

Organizations and Web Sites

Cabeza Prieta Natural History Association

http://cabezaprieta.org

Learn more about the plants and animals found in the Sonoran Desert.

Mission Churches of the Sonoran Desert

http://parentseyes.arizona.edu/missions

Read more about the missions settled in the Sonoran Desert.

National Museum of the American Indian

www.nmai.si.edu

View Native American art and items.

Places to Visit

San Xavier del Bac Mission

1950 W. San Xavier Road
Tucson, AZ 85746
(520) 294-2624
www.sanxaviermission.org/
This mission's church sits on Tohono O'odham land and still serves the Native American community.

Tumacácori National Historical Park

1891 E. Frontage Road
Tumacácori, AZ 85640
(520) 398-2341
www.nps.gov/tuma/
Visit the ruins of three Spanish missions.

Important Words

adobe (uh-DOH-bee) – a building material of clay mixed with straw that is dried in the sun and made into bricks

altar – a table used in religious ceremonies

claimed – took possession of

convert – to cause to accept different ideas or beliefs

mathematician (math-uh-muh-TI-shun) – a person who works with math

missionaries – people who work to convince other people to join their religion

nomadic – moving from place to place

presidios (preh-SEE-dee-ohz) – forts built by the Spanish

revolts – acts of rising up and fighting against a government or authority

Index

Page numbers in **bold** indicate illustrations

About the Author

Robin Lyon writes fiction and nonfiction books for children. She also works as an editor and Web designer.